THE WORLD OF ENERGY

Understanding
NUCLEAR
POWER

FIONA REYNOLDSON

Gareth Stevens
Publishing

Please visit our Web site, www.garethstevens.com. For a free color catalog of all our high-quality books, call toll free 1-800-542-2595 or fax 1-877-542-2596.

Library of Congress Cataloging-in-Publication Data

Reynoldson, Fiona.
 Understanding nuclear power / Fiona Reynoldson.
   p. cm. — (The world of energy)
 Includes index.
 ISBN 978-1-4339-4124-5 (library binding)
 1. Nuclear energy—Juvenile literature. I. Title.
 TK9148.R49 2011
 621.48'3—dc22

                               2010015847

This edition first published in 2011 by
Gareth Stevens Publishing
111 East 14th Street, Suite 349
New York, NY 10003

Copyright © 2011 Wayland/Gareth Stevens Publishing

Editorial Director: Kerri O'Donnell
Art Director: Haley Harasymiw

Photo Credits:
AEA Technology, Harwell: 5 top, 8 bottom, 14 right, 17 top, 18 top, 28 top, 29, 31, 33, 37, 41, 44, 45; Biofoto, Denmark: 22 right; British Nuclear Fuels: 6 right, 12, 13, 14 left, 15, 16, 19, 23, 30, 32 (Hodder Wayland Picture Library), 42; Corbis 10 (Bettmann), 11 (Bettmann); Ecoscene: 5 bottom, 27 (Close); EDF: 6 left, 34, 35; Olë Steen Hansen: 18 right; Mary Evans Picture Library: 8 top; Science Photo Library: 9 (Argon ne National Laboratory), 17 bottom (Martin Bond), 26 (Novosti), 28 bottom (Peter Menzel), 36 left (BSIP, RAGUET), 43 (Sandia National Laboratories); Shutterstock.com cover and 1 (Martin D. Vonka); Stockmarket: 21, 24, 39; U.S. Department of Energy: 22 left, 25, 26 left, 36 right, 40.

Printed in the China
CPSIA compliance information: Batch #WAS10GS: For further information contact Gareth Stevens, New York, New York at 1-800-542-2595.

CONTENTS

WHAT IS NUCLEAR POWER?

Introduction

Everything in the world, from water and stones to people and trees, is made up of elements. Two common elements are oxygen and hydrogen.

- Elements are made up of atoms.
- Each atom has a center called a nucleus.
- Each nucleus has protons and neutrons inside it.

The Elements

We tell one element from another by the number of protons in its nucleus. The lightest element is hydrogen. It has one proton. One of the heaviest elements is uranium. It has 92 protons.

Splitting the Atom

Protons and neutrons are tightly bound together in the nucleus of an atom. Splitting the atoms releases this "binding energy." The atoms of most elements are so tightly bound together that they cannot be split. But uranium is different. It can be split.

FACT FILE

Uranium atoms are big—they have 92 protons. They are unstable, and easy to split apart. The energy released when they split is enormous. This energy is called nuclear power. Splitting the atom is called nuclear fission.

...plitting the atom. A neutron hits a uranium nucleus. The nucleus absorbs the neutron. The nucleus is now so unstable it breaks up. This is called nuclear fission. ▶

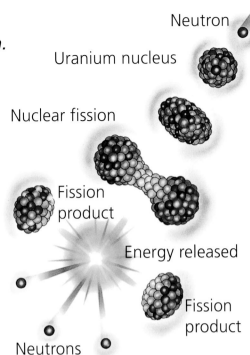

Neutron

Uranium nucleus

Nuclear fission

Fission product

Energy released

Fission product

Neutrons

A nuclear power plant. The energy released from splitting the atom can be used to make electricity. ▼

FACT FILE

RADIATION

An electric radiator radiates heat. A radio radiates radio waves. The sun radiates light. Energy is radiating around the world all the time, in the form of light and heat. Much of this energy does us good. However, the invisible radiation given out by uranium can damage cells in our bodies.

A uranium mine. Here the uranium is near the surface. This is called an open-pit mine. ▼

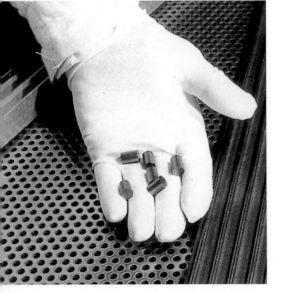

▲ *Uranium oxide pellets ready for use as fuel in a power plant.*

What Is Uranium?

Uranium is a grayish-white metal. It looks like steel but is two and a half times as heavy as steel

Uranium is dug from the earth. Long ago, uraniu was made far out in space when huge stars exploded. Fragments from these explosions (including uranium) formed planets such as Earth

Uranium Ores

Uranium is found mixed up with rocks. When it is mixed up like this it is called uranium ore. The most common uranium ores are called pitchblende and carnotite. The best uranium ore is found in Canada, the United States, and the Congo in Africa.

There are different types of uranium in the uranium ores. Two of these are:

- U238—the most common type
- U235—the most useful type.

Building nuclear power plants is very expensive. Africa has very few. In general, Australia uses water or coal power for its power plants. ▼

☐ Nuclear power

● Uranium mining

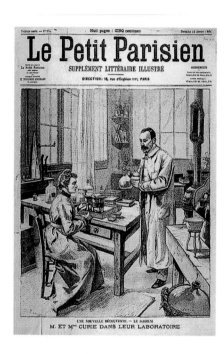

▲ *Marie Curie discovered two new elements that are radioactive, just as uranium is. These elements are radium and polonium.*

Discoveries

- In 1789, a German scientist named Martin Heinrich Klaproth discovered uranium oxide (impure uranium).
- In 1842, a French scientist, Eugene Peligot, discovered the pure element uranium.
- In 1892, another French scientist, Henri Becquerel, discovered that uranium was radioactive. It gives out invisible rays that affect things around it. For example, the invisible rays from a lump of uranium make a photographic plate dark, in the same way that light does.

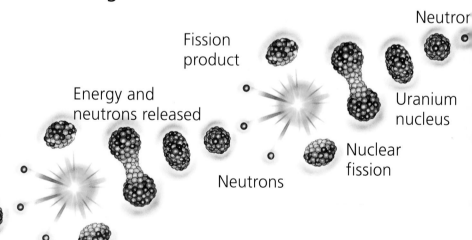

Neutron

Fission product

Energy and neutrons released

Uranium nucleus

Nuclear fission

Neutrons

Neutrons

Direction of reaction

Uranium nucleus

Neutrons

▲ *This diagram shows the chain reaction started when one neutron hits a uranium nucleus.*

▲ *This painting shows the first controlled nuclear chain reaction in 1942. The chain reaction is taking place inside the building on the right. The scientists are measuring what is happening inside the building. This work was led by an Italian scientist named Enrico Fermi. He was working at the University of Chicago in Illinois.*

A Nuclear Reactor

A nuclear chain reaction has to be carefully controlled. It is done inside a strong container. This container and its contents is called a nuclear reactor. It is often just called a reactor for short. The building on the right of the painting was the first nuclear reactor.

FACT FILE

Below are the places and dates when nuclear power was first used to make electricity.

- 1951—Idaho Falls, Idaho
- 1955—Obninsk, Russia
- 1956—Calder Hall, Cumbria, UK. This was the world's first commercial nuclear power plant.

Largest Nuclear Plant

The Palo Verde Nuclear Generating Station is the largest nuclear power plant in the United States. It took 12 years to build and cost $6 million. The plant can generate 3.2 gigawatts (GW) of power each year— enough electricity to supply four million people in Arizona and Southern California. The site's three pressurized water reactors (PWRs) all function as separate units.

▲ *The Palo Verde Nuclear Generating Station began working in 1988. It is located in Wintersburg, Arizona, in a desert area.*

FACT FILE

ENERGY PRODUCED:

1 ton of uranium
= 25,000 tons of coal
= 4.2 million gallons
(15.9 million L) of oil

Water Solution

Nuclear power plants need a lot of water to cool the reactors (see page 31). Palo Verde is the only nuclear power plant in the world that is located far away from a large body of water such as a lake, so it must find its water from somewhere else.

Palo Verde uses evaporated water from treated sewage plants in the area. This water is stored and treated again in a reservoir at the plant site. Around 20 billion gallons (76 billion L) of water is needed each year to cool the reactors.

Each nuclear reactor at the Palo Verde power plant works as a separate unit. The concrete dome covering each reactor is 4 feet (1.2 m) thick. ▼

Getting Uranium from Uranium Ore

Uranium ore is rock with uranium in it. The pure uranium has to be separated from the rock.

Getting the Uranium—Method One

The uranium ore is crushed and dissolved in acid What is left is:

- unwanted rock
- uranium oxide, which can be changed into uranium and used as a fuel.

Getting the Uranium—Method Two

- Two boreholes are drilled down to the uranium ore in the ground.
- Solvent is pumped down one hole.
- The solvent dissolves the uranium in the ore.
- The solvent (containing the uranium) comes up the second hole to the surface.

Plutonium

Some nuclear reactors and nuclear weapons use plutonium as a fuel. Plutonium is a very rare element. Most plutonium is made from uranium.

A scientist working on the fuel cans. These cans encase the uranium fuel rods. The cans are put in the reactor (see the diagram on page 13). ▼

FACT FILE

Plutonium gives out very high energy radiation. It is very dangerous but useful. Advantages of plutonium reactors are:

- they are very reliable for a long time, and
- they are lightweight.

Plutonium is used as a fuel in space probes. It used to be used in pacemakers for hearts.

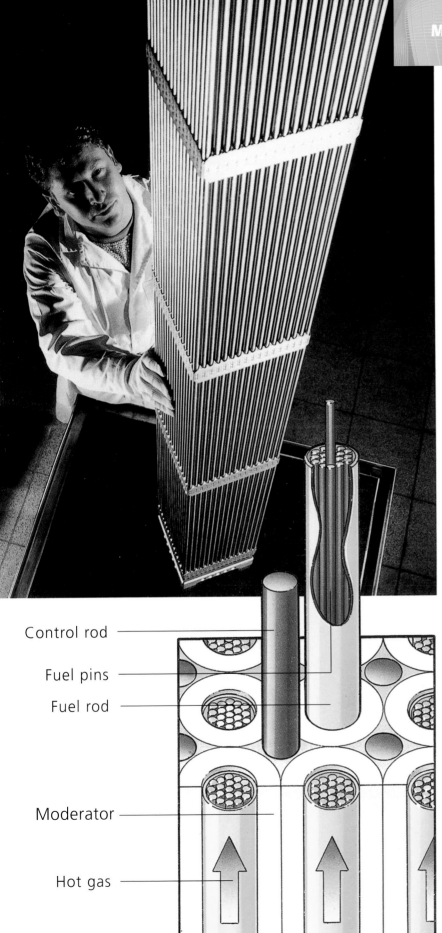

Control rod

Fuel pins

Fuel rod

Moderator

Hot gas

◀ *This is a fuel assembly. Each assembly contains 298 uranium fuel pins inside fuel rods.*

◀ *This is a drawing of what is inside the fuel assembly in the photograph above. The moderator can be graphite, light (ordinary) water, or heavy water. The job of the moderator is to slow down the neutrons so that they are more likely to cause fission.*

Reusing Old Fuel

Gradually, the fuel in the reactors gives out less and less heat. But there is still usable uranium in the old fuel. It just has to be recycled to get the uranium out. This recycling is called reprocessing.

It is worth reprocessing old fuel. One ton of reprocessed fuel gives as much energy as 20,000 tons of oil.

▲ Old fuel rods produce a blue glow when they are in water.

◄ Old fuel cooling in storage ponds at a reprocessing plant in the UK. Most of the world's reprocessing is done in France, the UK, Japan, and Germany.

◀ *Inside a reprocessing plant. Fuel rods that have cooled down are being broken open to get the old fuel out.*

Nuclear Waste

Nuclear power plants have to deal with their own waste (apart from old fuel, which is dealt with in a reprocessing plant). This waste is divided into three groups:

- low-level waste, such as workers' clothes
- intermediate-level waste, such as empty fuel cans
- high-level waste, such as liquid chemicals.

The group each type of waste goes into depends on how radioactive it is.

FACT FILE

One way of describing radioactivity is in half lives. A half life is the time it takes for half the atoms of an element to decay. Uranium 238 has a half life of four and a half billion years!

Reprocessing in France

The Areva NC la Hague reprocessing plant is the world's largest LWR (Light Water Reactor) reprocessing plant. It reprocesses old nuclear fuel for France and for 27 other countries. It can reprocess up to 1,900 tons (1,700 tonnes) of old fuel per year. The old fuel arrives at the plant. It is stored underwater for several years until it has cooled down and is less radioactive.

The Areva NC nuclear reprocessing plant is near Cherbourg in northern France. ▼

Making New Fuel

When they are cool, the fuel assemblies are broken open. The fuel rods are cut into 1.2 inch (3 cm) lengths. They are put into acid to dissolve and then separated into uranium, plutonium, and waste products.

▲ *Reprocessed uranium can be handled safely. These are new fuel rods for an AGR (Advanced Gas-cooled Reactor).*

A view of the Areva NC plant at night. ▼

◀ *A scientist checks radiation levels in the fields near Hunterston B nuclear power plant in Scotland.*

Affecting the Surrounding World

Burning coal and gas in power plants causes air pollution. Nuclear power plants do not cause air pollution. But some of the nuclear waste will be radioactive for millions of years. This is very dangerous.

Protection

The inside of nuclear power plants is checked all the time. Workers wear special meters that record the radiation around them. The air is checked, too. If any radioactive gas leaks out, it is known immediately.

▲ *This badge says: Nuclear Power? No Thanks! Danish people refused to allow their government to build nuclear power plants.*

Some countries used to dump nuclear waste in the sea or in lakes, or buried it in the ground. This happened in some parts of the former Soviet Union. Now there are lakes that are very contaminated by nuclear waste. A person could receive a deadly dose of radiation just by standing by the lake.

A worker at a nuclear power plant checks his radiation monitor before he enters a radioactive area. ▼

FACT FILE

Some countries such as Denmark feel that nuclear power is so dangerous they will not allow any nuclear power plants to be built. Other countries such as France and Japan are continuing to build nuclear power plants.

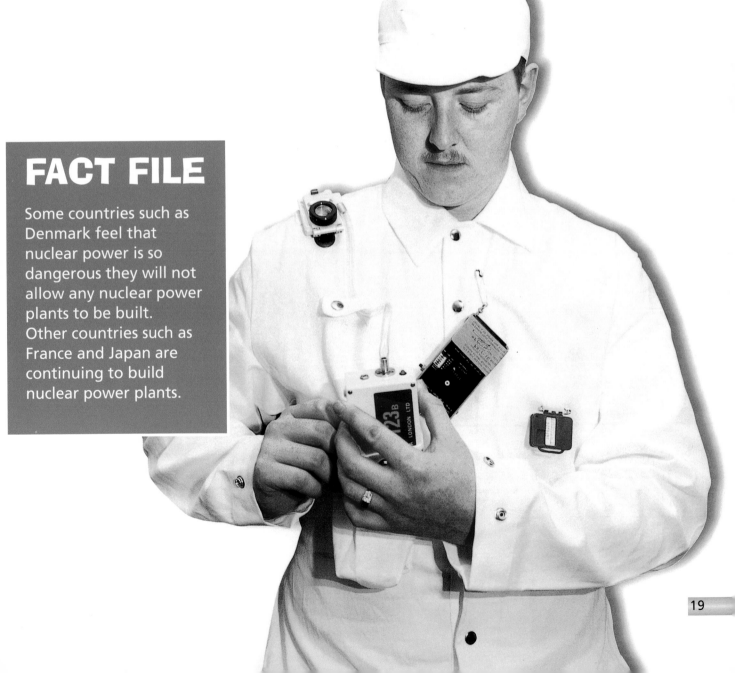

Nuclear Power in War

The first use of nuclear power was in war. The first atomic bomb was dropped on Hiroshima in Japan in 1945. Most of Hiroshima was destroyed. About 100,000 people were killed. Three days later, a second bomb was dropped on the city of Nagasaki. Nearly as many people were killed.

Radioactive materials make three different types of radiation. These are called alpha, beta, and gamma. Alpha and beta radiation are particles. Gamma radiation is a wave, more like light. Alpha, beta, and gamma rays can go through solid objects (see the diagram below). ▼

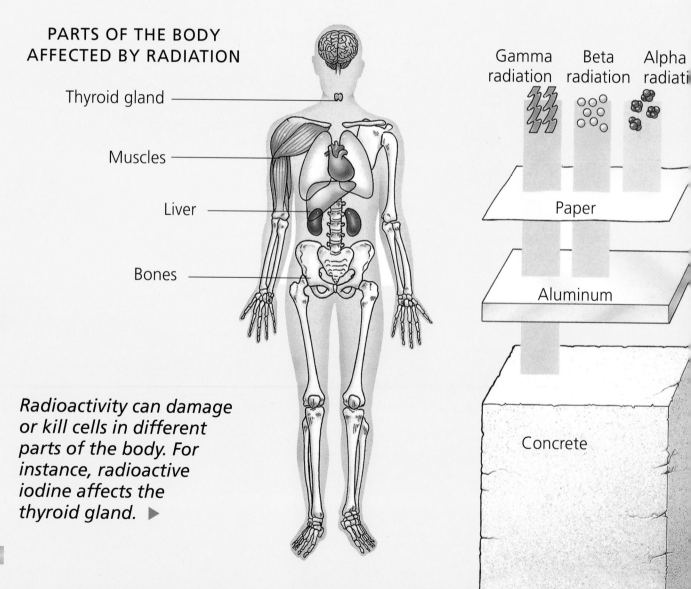

PARTS OF THE BODY AFFECTED BY RADIATION

Thyroid gland

Muscles

Liver

Bones

Radioactivity can damage or kill cells in different parts of the body. For instance, radioactive iodine affects the thyroid gland. ▶

Gamma radiation

Beta radiation

Alpha radiation

Paper

Aluminum

Concrete

◀ *A nuclear explosion can destroy a whole city in seconds. People who survive the explosion may become sick later.*

Radiation Sickness

Radiation can cause ulcers and burns. It can damage bone marrow and cause cancer. Radiation can also damage unborn children, through harming cells in the parents' bodies.

FACT FILE

Luminous watch dials used to be painted with radioactive paint. Workers licked their paintbrushes to make a fine point. Many of those workers got mouth cancer.

Transporting Nuclear Fuels

There are two types of nuclear fuel to transport:

- new nuclear fuel, from the processing plant to the power plants, and
- old nuclear fuel, from the power plants to reprocessing plants.

Nuclear containers must never leak. The radioactive fuel could cause terrible damage. In the U.S.A., old fuel is transported in enormously strong casks on the railroads. ▼

Old fuel is transported by ship from Sweden to the UK or France for reprocessing. ▶

These flasks contain old fuel from British nuclear power plants. They are being transported to the reprocessing plant at Sellafield in Cumbria, UK. ▶

Nuclear Containers

The containers are called flasks. They are very strong and expensive.

- They are made of steel.
- They cost up to $1.6 million each.
- They can survive being dropped from 30 feet (9 m) to a flat surface, and from 3 feet (1 m) onto a sharp point.
- They can withstand a fire at 14,432° F (8,000° C) for half an hour.

FACT FILE

A nuclear flask was tested in the UK. A diesel engine and three train carriages were crashed into it at a speed of 100 mph (160 km/h). The only thing unharmed was the flask.

Storing Nuclear Waste

Waste such as ashes from fires is safe. But waste from nuclear power is very dangerous, because it is radioactive. It cannot just be buried in the ground without being sealed in. The radiation would escape and contaminate water supplies.

Low-level and intermediate-level waste is sealed in containers and stored above ground. High-level (very radioactive) waste is often set in hard glass bricks and buried underground.

An underground nuclear waste storage site in the U.S.A. ▼

Burying Nuclear Waste at Sea

All nuclear waste that is buried now, is buried on land. In the future, it may be buried at sea.

In 1,000 years, the metal waste containers would rust and crumble. The radioactive waste would leak out. But scientists believe that the fine ocean mud would stop radiation from spreading.

▲ *A technician uses a robotic arm and safety cabinet to handle radioactive waste at a reprocessing plant.*

The diagram shows how nuclear waste might be buried at sea. Each stage from 1 to 4 is designed to stop radiation from leaking into the seabed. ▶

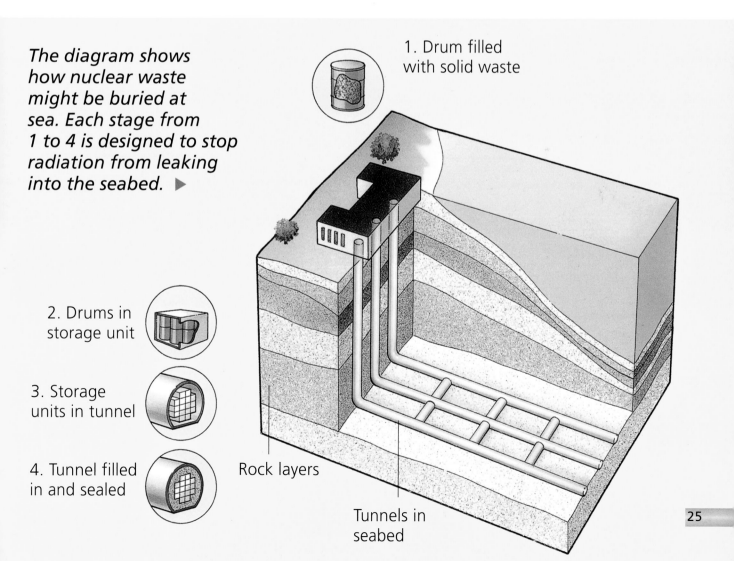

1. Drum filled with solid waste

2. Drums in storage unit

3. Storage units in tunnel

4. Tunnel filled in and sealed

Rock layers

Tunnels in seabed

A computer simulation shows how far radioactive material from the accident at Chernobyl had spread around the world ten days after the explosion. ▼

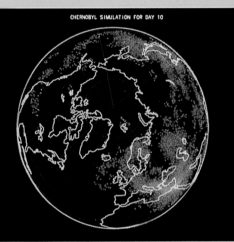

CHERNOBYL SIMULATION FOR DAY 10

An aerial view of the damaged reactor at Chernobyl. People living near Chernobyl received the highest radiation doses and have suffered serious health problems. ▶

Nuclear Accidents

There have been nuclear accidents in the United States and in the UK. However, the worst nuclear accident, so far, was on April 26, 1986, at Chernobyl in the Ukraine. One of the four reactors exploded and caught fire.

What Happened at Chernobyl?

Scientists were conducting a test on the reactor. The power output began to rise so the operators began to lower the control rods. But they could not do it quickly enough. The fuel began to overheat. There was water inside the reactor that was used for cooling. As the fuel overheated, this water turned to steam. The steam reacted with the graphite and exploded. The water and hot fuel mixed even more. There were more explosions—so powerful that they blew the 1,120-ton (1,000-tonne) lid off the reactor. Heavy radioactive material fell around Chernobyl, and lighter radioactive material was carried away by the wind.

◀ As far away as the UK, some sheep were contaminated by radioactive particles that fell on them and on the grass they ate.

▲ *A nuclear power plant is run and monitored from the control room.*

What Is a Power Plant?

A power plant uses fuel to make water boil. This makes steam. The steam turns the shaft of a turbine. The spinning shaft transfers its energy to a generator. The generator converts the movement into electricity.

Generators work by turning a magnet inside a coil of wire. The magnetic field pulls the electrons around and around the coil, pushing them out at one end and pulling them in at the other. This movement makes electricity.

Steam rises from the cooling towers at a nuclear power plant in California. The condensers that change the steam back to water need up to 53 million gallons (200 million L) of water an hour. ▶

The generators at a nuclear power plant. The pipes are carrying steam.

Differences Between Power Plants

There are two important differences between nuclear power plants and fossil fuel power plants.

- Nuclear power plants use nuclear fuel (a uranium-based fuel). Fossil fuel power plants use coal, oil, or gas.
- Nuclear fuel gives out heat due to fission. There is no burning. Fossil fuels have to be burned to give out heat.

FACT FILE

There are about 438 nuclear power plants in the world. There are two types:
- thermal reactors and
- fast reactors.

Thermal Reactors

There are many different designs of thermal reactor. These are a few of them:

- PWR (Pressurized Water Reactor)
- AGR (Advanced Gas-cooled Reactor)
- BWR (Boiling Water Reactor)
- CANDU (Canadian Deuterium Uranium).
- Magnox (now obsolete).

Coolants

Coolants are used to carry heat away from the reactor. Different thermal reactors use different coolants. Some use a gas coolant. Others use a liquid coolant.

A PWR (pressurize water reactor) in Germany. The dome-shaped building is the reactor room. ▼

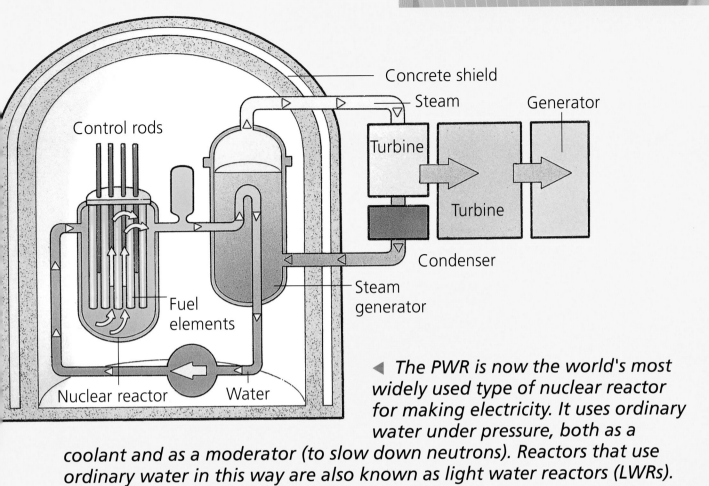

Control rods

Concrete shield

Steam

Generator

Turbine

Turbine

Fuel
elements

Steam
generator

Condenser

Nuclear reactor

Water

◄ *The PWR is now the world's most widely used type of nuclear reactor for making electricity. It uses ordinary water under pressure, both as a coolant and as a moderator (to slow down neutrons). Reactors that use ordinary water in this way are also known as light water reactors (LWRs).*

Fuels

Most thermal reactors use enriched uranium fuel. This contains more U-235 than is found in natural uranium. Boosting the amount of U-235 increases the chances of nuclear fission (see page 5). More fission produces more heat, which produces more electricity.

Electricity is sent down cables from the power plant, which carry it to towns and factories. ▶

Advantages of Fast Reactors

Fast reactors make better use of uranium than thermal reactors do.

- Fast reactors use a mixture of uranium and plutonium as fuel. The uranium waste from thermal reactors can be used in fast reactors.
- A fast reactor can change about half of the heat it makes into electricity. A thermal reactor only changes about one third of the heat it makes into electricity.

Making More Fuel

Look at the diagram on page 33. The core of a fast reactor can be surrounded by a blanket of uranium-238. This is hit many times by neutrons. It is slowly changed into plutonium. Fast reactors make more fuel than they use.

◀ *The UK's first fast reactor, at Dounreay in Scotland, opened in 1975. It is being phased out and is set to shut down by 2036.*

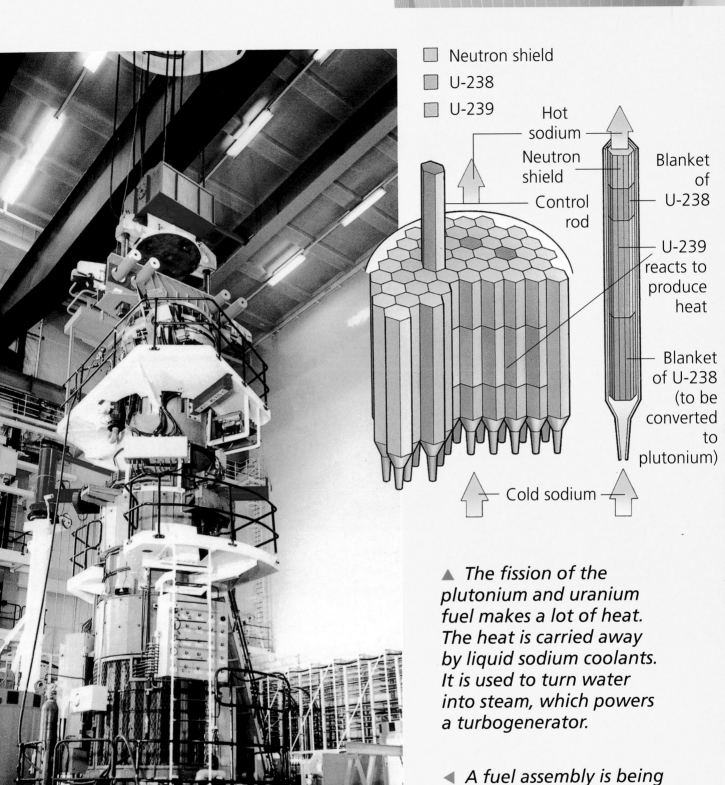

Neutron shield
U-238
U-239

Hot sodium
Neutron shield
Control rod
Blanket of U-238
U-239 reacts to produce heat
Blanket of U-238 (to be converted to plutonium)
Cold sodium

▲ The fission of the plutonium and uranium fuel makes a lot of heat. The heat is carried away by liquid sodium coolants. It is used to turn water into steam, which powers a turbogenerator.

◄ A fuel assembly is being moved to the reactor at Dounreay.

The Superphénix fast reactor near Lyon in France started operating in 1986. The reactor core was in the tall building. It was cooled by 5,600 tons (5,000 tonnes) of liquid sodium. ▶

Fuel pellets of uranium and plutonium put in steel tubes in the core of the reactor of Superphénix. ▼

Superphénix and Change

Superphénix was built between 1974 and 1986 to produce electricity. It was given a license to do this. (All nuclear power plants have to have a license to make sure they work safely.) In 1994, the license for Superphénix was changed, and it stopped making electricity to sell. It was used for scientific research instead. But this license was stopped in 1997, when the French decided to shut down Superphénix permanently.

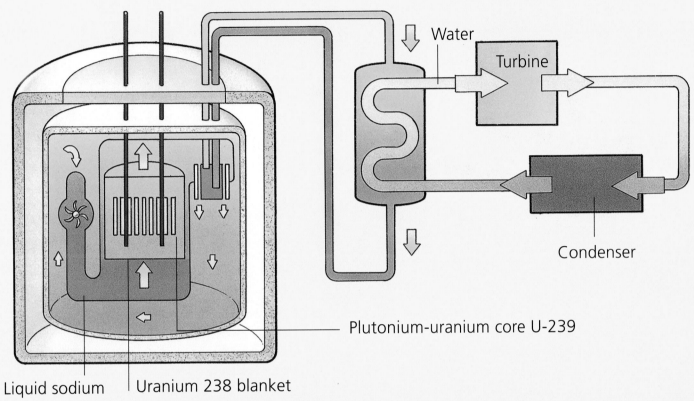

Water

Turbine

Condenser

Plutonium-uranium core U-239

Liquid sodium

Uranium 238 blanket

Shutting Down a Nuclear Reactor

The French said that the Superphénix was too expensive to run. It operated for the last time in December 1996, but it takes some time to shut down a fast nuclear reactor. All the 5,600 tons (5,000 tonnes) of liquid sodium coolant had to be drained slowly away, as the fuel was removed. This process took many years to complete.

▲ *The reactor had several layers around it to stop any radioactive material from escaping. The whole reactor was then encased in a thick concrete shield.*

Radioactivity and Cancer

Radioactivity can be used to detect or kill cancer cells in the human body.

Doctors have found ways of using radiation. Treating patients with radiation is called radiotherapy. Rays of radiation can reach deep inside the body. They can kill cancer cells without harming the flesh they pass through on the way. This allows doctors to kill cancer cells in areas such as the brain, where surgery is too dangerous.

▲ *This laboratory in the United States makes radioactive materials for medicines, industry, research, and farming.*

A patient is having a PET scan. PET scans are used to find cancers in the body. ▼

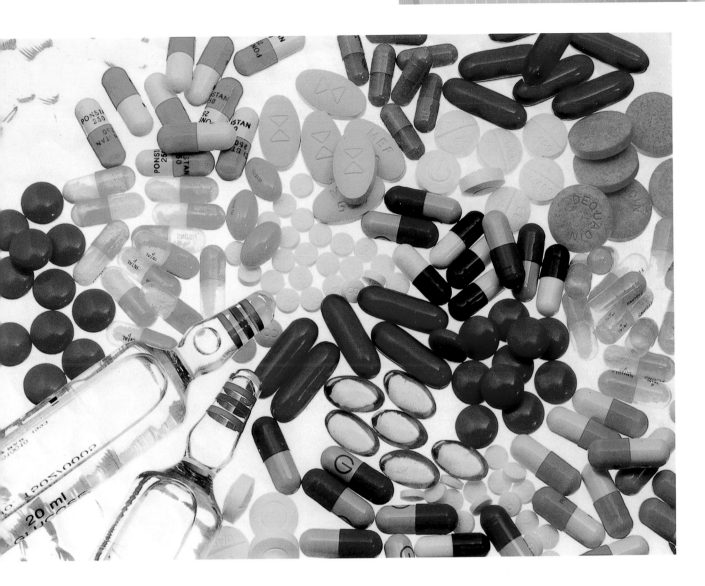

▲ *Radioactive material can be injected or taken as a tablet. They can show how well an organ, such as the liver, is working.*

Radioactive Markers

Some weak radioactive materials can be injected into one part of the body. These are called markers. They can be tracked around the body.

Radioactive materials can also be put into a food or drug. Then scientists can study where the food or the drug is going in the body.

Nuclear-Powered Vehicles

Small nuclear reactors can power vehicles such as submarines and spacecraft. They have some advantages over other fuels, such as diesel.

Advantages of Nuclear Power

- Nuclear-powered engines use less fuel and do not use up oxygen.
- Submarines can stay underwater for months.

Disadvantages of Nuclear Power

- Nuclear technology is very expensive.
- It is difficult and dangerous to operate.

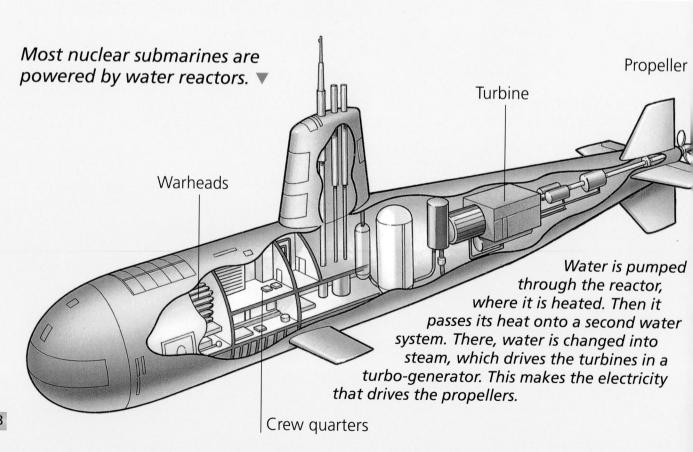

Most nuclear submarines are powered by water reactors. ▼

Propeller

Turbine

Warheads

Water is pumped through the reactor, where it is heated. Then it passes its heat onto a second water system. There, water is changed into steam, which drives the turbines in a turbo-generator. This makes the electricity that drives the propellers.

Crew quarters

▲ *Nuclear submarines can stay under the water for much longer than diesel-powered submarines can.*

Nuclear Power in Space

Spacecraft carry instruments such as cameras and radios, which are powered by electricity made from sunlight. This is called solar power. When traveling farther than Mars, there is not enough sunlight to make electricity. Nuclear power could help power spacecraft to planets far from Earth. But many people think this is too dangerous for astronauts. More research is needed to ensure safety.

Nuclear Weapons

One pound (0.45 kg) of matter changed into energy equals enough energy to explode 22 billion pounds (10 billion kg) of normal explosive.

▲ *This U.S. nuclear bomb has about 6,000 parts in it.*

The first nuclear bombs worked by ramming enough plutonium together to make sure that lots of fission took place. This released so much energy that a huge explosion happened. (See the photo on page 21.)

A nuclear missile is a rocket with a nuclear bomb on top. Large missiles have up to three rockets. Each rocket powers the bomb to the target. Some nuclear missiles explode when they hit the target. Others explode in the air above the target. ▼

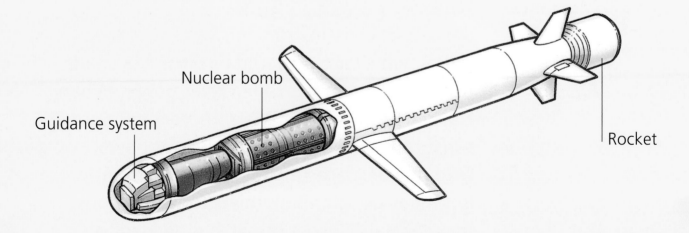

Guidance system

Nuclear bomb

Rocket

Triggering Explosion in Nuclear Weapons

There are two types of nuclear weapon:

- a fission weapon—ordinary explosives are used to ram pieces of plutonium together so that they will explode
- a fusion weapon—a hydrogen bomb works by fusing nuclei rather than splitting them. But a hydrogen bomb needs a fission bomb to trigger it and make the tremendous heat needed for nuclei to fuse together. This produces even more energy.

◀ *A technician studies plutonium waste at a fast reactor site. Old fuel from the reactor is separated into plutonium, uranium, and waste. Some plutonium is used to make nuclear weapons.*

FACT FILE

Critical mass is the minimum amount of material needed to speed up the rate of fissions so that all the energy comes out very quickly, causing an explosion. These explosions are enormous.

FACT FILE

A tiny amount of two rare types of hydrogen (deuterium and tritium) would make enough electricity to last one person a whole lifetime.

If all electricity came from nuclear power, the radioactive waste from one person's lifetime use of electricity would be the size of the ball in the photograph. ▼

Fission and Fusion

So far, scientists have used fission to make nucle power (see page 5). In the future, they may use fusion instead.

Uncontrolled Fusion

If hydrogen nuclei are slammed together hard enough, they combine. This makes helium plus a big release of energy. So far, scientists have no been able to control this energy. It has turned into a hydrogen bomb.

What scientists need to do is to make a reactor where nuclear fusion can be controlled.

The Problems

Nuclear fusion needs incredible heat to make the nuclei move fast enough to hit each other hard enough to fuse together. This only happens in stars such as the sun.

Scientists have made a reactor that works like the center of the sun. But it will only work for a few seconds at a time.

Fusion reactors such
s this one in the U.S.A.
se deuterium and
ritium. Particles are
being fired at a pellet
f deuterium and
ritium. This causes
usion. The electricity
lashing over the water
s a dramatic side effect.

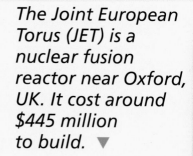

The Joint European Torus (JET) is a nuclear fusion reactor near Oxford, UK. It cost around $445 million to build. ▼

FACT FILE

Fusion reactors like JET are called tokamaks. Tokamak comes from Russian words meaning doughnut-shaped. That is the shape of the reactor core (see the diagram on page 45).

JET

The Joint European Torus (JET) nuclear fusion reactor started work in 1983.

How Does It Work?

The deuterium and tritium fuel is held in place by two magnetic fields. One magnetic field is made by 32 magnets. The other magnetic field is made by an enormous electric current. This electric current, plus radio waves, heats the fuel to over 212 million degrees F (100 million degrees Celsius). This super-hot material is called plasma. Inside it, the nuclei crash into each other and fuse together.

▲ *This is an experimental fusion reactor. Scientists have to get the reactor to make more energy than it uses up.*

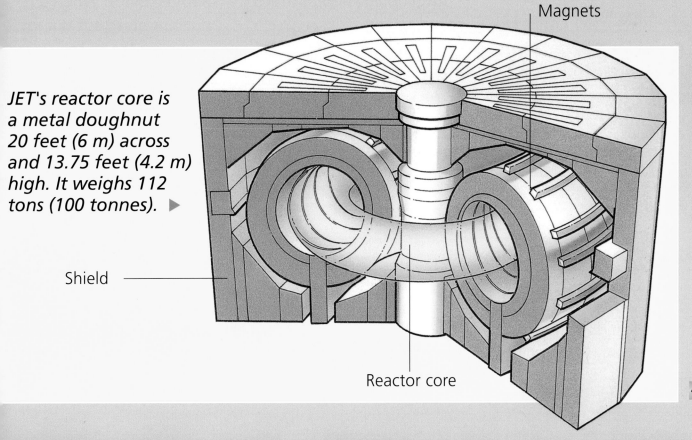

Magnets

JET's reactor core is a metal doughnut 20 feet (6 m) across and 13.75 feet (4.2 m) high. It weighs 112 tons (100 tonnes). ▶

Shield

Reactor core

GLOSSARY

Advanced Gas-cooled Reactor (AGR) A type of thermal nuclear reactor.

Alpha particle A particle flung out by a decaying atom. It is too large to go through a sheet of paper.

Beta particle A particle flung out by a decaying atom. It can go through a sheet of paper but cannot go through a sheet of aluminum.

Condenser A machine for changing gas into liquid—for example, steam into water.

Control rod A rod lowered into a nuclear reactor to slow down or stop nuclear reactions.

Deuterium A rare type of hydrogen.

Fast reactor A type of nuclear reactor that uses fast-moving neutrons to make nuclear fission.

Gamma ray An electromagnetic wave given out by a nuclear reaction.

It can go through paper and aluminum but is stopped by thick concrete.

Heavy water Water that contains deuterium instead of ordinary hydrogen.

Light Water Reactor (LWR) A type of pressurized water nuclear reactor.

Magnetic field The space around a magnet where the force of the magnet can be felt.

Magnox An early type of gas-cooled nuclear reactor.

Moderator A material inside a thermal reactor that slows down neutrons.

Nuclear fission Splitting a nucleus.

Nuclear fusion The joining together of two or more nuclei.

Nuclear radiation Energy given out by nuclear reactions.

Nuclear reactor A structure where nuclear chain reactions take place.

Nucleus The particle or particles at the center of a atom, e.g. neutrons. The plural of nucleus is nuclei.

Particle A tiny part of something.

Plutonium A highly radioactive element used as a fuel in some nuclear reactors.

Pressurized Water Reactor (PWR) The most widely used type of thermal nuclear reactor.

Radioactivity When a nucleus gives out energy.

Solvent A liquid you can dissolve something in.

Tokamak A type of nuclear fusion reactor.

Tritium A rare type of hydrogen.

Turbine A shaft turned by water or gas.

Turbogenerator An electricity generator driven by a turbine.

Uranium An element used as a fuel in nuclear reactors

Further Reading

The Energy Debate: The Pros and Cons of Nuclear Power
by Ewan McLeish
Rosen Central, 2007

Energy Today: Nuclear Power
by Richard Hantula
Chelsea House Publications, 2010

Powering the Future: New Energy Technologies
by Eva Thaddeus
University of New Mexico Press, 2010

Web Sites

http://home.clara.net/darvill/altenerg/nuclear.htm

http://library.thinkquest.org/3471/nuclear_energy.html

http://science.howstuffworks.com/nuclear-power.htm

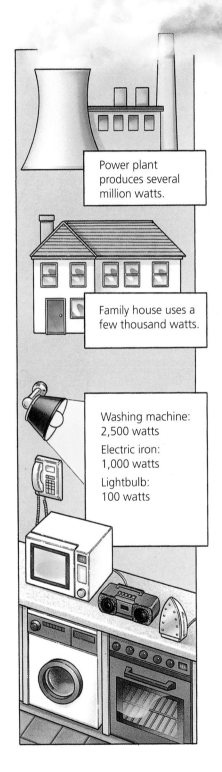

Power plant produces several million watts.

Family house uses a few thousand watts.

Washing machine: 2,500 watts

Electric iron: 1,000 watts

Lightbulb: 100 watts

ENERGY CONSUMPTION
The use of energy is measured in joules per second, or watts. Different machines use up different amounts of energy. The diagram on the right gives a few examples. ▶

INDEX